Copyright © 2025 Grow Grit Press LLC. All rights reserved. No part of this book may be reproduced in any form without permission in writing from the publisher. Please send bulk order requests to info@ninjalifehacks.tv

Paperback ISBN: 978-1-63731-972-7
Hardcover ISBN: 978-1-63731-974-1
eBook ISBN: 978-1-63731-973-4

Printed and bound in the USA.
NinjaLifeHacks.tv

Ninja Life Hacks®
by Mary Nhin

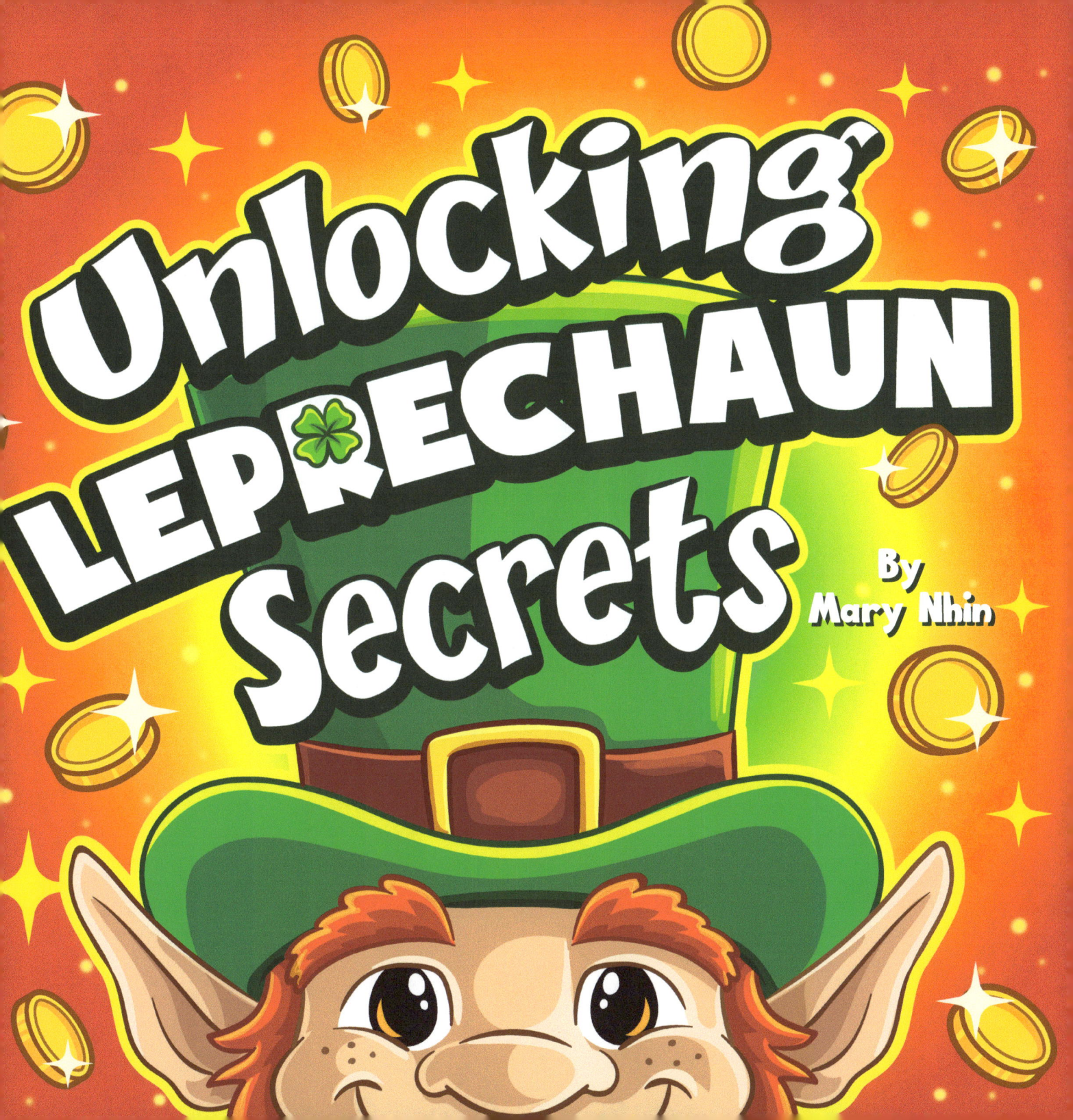

Today, I'm on a mission,
To uncover a **secret** so bold.
I've heard that leprechauns conceal,
A tale about their gold.

Liam the leprechaun says, "Let's try it!"
His spirit is alive with delight.
He studies the map with renewed focus,
Hoping to find the gold **tonight**.

He spots the tree shaped like a duck,
And the rock that looks like Aunt Patty.
With every step, he gains more luck,
Feeling brave and oh so **happy**.

I love to hear from my readers. Email me your feedback or thoughts on what my next story should be at info@ninjalifehacks.tv

Yours truly, Mary

@marynhin   @GrowGrit
#NinjaLifeHacks

Mary Nhin   Ninja Life Hacks

Ninja Life Hacks

@officialninjalifehacks

www.ingramcontent.com/pod-product-compliance
Lightning Source LLC
Chambersburg PA
CBHW041711160426
43209CB00018B/1804